G000255268

Marx for Today

Lindsey German, Chris Nineham, James Meadway and
Katherine Connelly

a **COUNTERFIRE** publication

Marx for Today

First published in Great Britain in 2015 by Counterfire, Unit 206, 39-41 North Road, N7 9DP.
Cover design and layout: Matt Bonner and Feyzi Ismail

ISBN 978-1-907899-04-1

A catalogue record for this book is available from the British Library.

Printed and bound in Great Britain.

Contents

1. Marx and his Times

Lindsey German*

My aim in this talk is to try to locate Karl Marx in his time, to look at some of the main events in his life and the way in which his ideas developed, and to draw a few conclusions which I think are relevant for today.

I will start with a couple of photographs of Marx. The first one [Fig. 1] is Marx as a respectable Victorian gentleman, perhaps the image that people have of Marx, the man who sat in the British Museum for years writing *Capital*. (As his mother said, writing about capital rather than making it. This was a constant gripe of the Marx family, who didn't entirely approve of what he was doing.)

The second is what he was like as a young man, in the late 1830s, which shows a very different Marx, very much the revolutionary [Fig. 2]. It's important to remember that he was always a revolutionary and always very keen on the ideas of revolution, as I hope I will be able to show.

The third is one of my favourite pictures of him, Marx on Hampstead Heath with Frederick Engels - who was his lifelong friend and collaborator and who sacrificed much of his life to make sure that Marx could write - and his three daughters, Laura, Eleanor and Jenny [Fig. 3]. His three surviving children were all daughters, although he had several other children who died in infancy.

People often talk about Marx as a genius, as someone who had a tremendous ability not just to write about economics but to distil the essence of what was going on in society. When he died, Engels said Marx was a genius, he said that he never had any problem playing second fiddle

* This is a transcript of a speech given by Lindsey German at the Marx in a Day event on 7 February 2015.

Figure 1

Figure 2

Figure 3

to Marx because that was a great place to be. He said 'Marx could have done anything that I did, but there were many things that Marx did that I could not have done.'

One of his biographers, David Riazanov, who was an extremely impressive Russian thinker who wrote a book about him round about a hundred years ago, said:

> To really determine the magnitude of the genius, one must first ascertain the antedating achievements, the degree of intellectual development of society, the social forms into which this genius was born, and from which he drew his psychological and physical sustenance.

When we think about the influences on Marx, we have to think chiefly of two things. The first was the French Revolution, the great overthrow of the aristocracy and the monarchy in France at the end of the eighteenth century and the ushering in of the ideas, most famously, of liberty, equality and fraternity, but also of change, of a society which was based on ideas of democracy. Marx was born in 1818, in Trier in the part of Germany called the Rhineland, which was itself occupied by Napoleon after the French Revolution and was very much influenced by these sorts of ideas. His family was originally a Jewish family but his father had broken with Judaism. Marx came from an incredibly fertile intellectual background, and a very liberal one, in which the ideas of the Enlightenment, of rational scientific thought, were of great importance.

The second thing which influenced him was the Industrial Revolution; the revolution which started in this country and which transformed the economy and created the factory system and the industrial working class. Indeed, when he became friends with Engels, one of Engels' contributions to Marx's thinking was in his experience of the industrial working class. Engels came from a factory-owning family in the Rhineland, but they owned a factory in Manchester. Engels spent quite a lot of his youth and much of his middle age working in Manchester in the factory and it was there that he first came across the working class and the Chartist movement. He was in the north of England just after the great general strike of 1842, and it was this experience which imbued Engels and Marx was a sense of the new working class.

It's often said of Marx, and I think it's a very fair point, that there were three different forces driving his thinking: German philosophy, English political economy and French socialism. The first two are dealt with elsewhere. So-called French Socialism was what we would now called Utopian Socialism (it's probably a slight exaggeration to say it was French as the Utopian Socialists included an Englishman called Robert Owen, who formed the Grand National Consolidated Trade Union, but it was mainly French.) Marx and Engels always admired the Utopian Socialists and agreed that they owed them a debt for developing socialism, but they regarded their socialism as limited in its ability to transform the world.

Engels in his book *Socialism: Utopian and Scientific*, explained that for the Utopians, 'socialism is the expression of absolute truth, reason and justice, and needs only to be discovered to conquer the world by virtue of its own power.' In other words, the Utopian Socialists said that you just have to say how awful society is for people to rise up and transform it. They also believed that the working class was the most oppressed class and which therefore had to be liberated, if necessary by the benevolent efforts of people like them.

Marx was very critical of this. He said that you can't just have a moral objection to capitalism; the working class is oppressed and it is exploited, but it is a class which has the power to transform its situation and bring about revolution. In fact, he said the working class is the only class which can rid itself of the muck of ages, as he called it, the rottenness of capitalist society, class society, and begin to create society anew.

While Marx and Engels were therefore very favourable towards the Utopians, they also believed that their immature theories, as they called them, corresponded to an early stage of capitalist production. In other words, you could first see the horror of that production, but it's only later that you would see the working class organising through trade unions and strikes.

In addition to these currents of thought, there was of course the actuality of revolution. By the late 1840s in Europe, there was widespread famine and unrest. Marx and Engels were always actually part of an organisation - even in the 1850s when they didn't really have much of an organisation, they had a kind of informal group, but in the 1840s they became connected with a group called the League of the Just, which later became known as the Communist League. It was for them that Marx was asked to write *The Communist Manifesto* - which apart from the Bible I think is the most widely read and widely sold book that there has ever been - and although Marx missed his deadline a couple of times and got a rather stern note from them, the *Manifesto* came out just as Europe was erupting in revolution. There were revolutions from Naples and Sicily, to the south of France to Germany. The revolutionaries would not have had a chance to read the *Manifesto* before the revolutions started, but it was very much a product of its time.

The Communist Manifesto is, strangely to us, quite enthusiastic about capitalism, because it sees capitalism as destroying the old ways of organising, all the old religions and the old feudal order. This was why Marx was so keen on the 1848 revolutions, which he then believed would themselves be rapidly superseded by an organised working class which would establish socialism and then communism.

One of the great tragedies of Marx's life was that the 1848 revolutions were not successful. In France, the revolution was eventually drowned in blood, because the new bourgeoisie - the new capitalist class - would rather stick with the existing order than allow the working class to take a leading role. This was repeated around the whole of Europe, particularly in Germany, where Marx was very critical of the revolutionaries. Marx himself was editor of a paper called the *Neue Rheinische Zeitung* (known as *The Organ of Democracy*) which he edited in Cologne, where he and Engels were based, during the 1848 revolutions. They regarded themselves as on the extreme left wing of this democratic revolution, which they then hoped would lead to a workers' revolution. Engels said in 1848 that 'the executioner stands at the door' - in other words, the working class is waiting to take over from the bourgeoisie, but as one of the scholars of Marx, Hal Draper, said 'the bourgeoisie refused to open that door'.

1848 was absolutely formative in Marx's and Engels' minds. Marx and Engels always referred all the subsequent things they did and how they judged things was always done on the basis of 1848, just as the Russian revolutionaries would constantly refer back to the French Revolution. In the long period of reaction and defeat after 1848, Marx came to London as a political exile, and Engels went to work in Manchester for the family factory, and supported Marx. There are many letters between Marx and Engels about the Marx family's finances, pleas for money in response to which Engels would send a case of champagne and claret. In 1859 they couldn't afford a Christmas tree, but they did get the champagne from Engels. Engels kept the family going financially and was like a second father to Marx's daughters.

Both Marx and Engels tried to keep abreast of what was going on politically, but it was very difficult. In the 1850s, the Chartists, the great revolutionary movement up to 1848 - or sections of them - still kept going but essentially it was a very hard time. Marx did demonstrate a few times over Sunday closing, which was a big issue, as it was the only time the working class had to shop, and he nearly got arrested for it.

By the beginning of the 1860s though, things began to change again. In 1860, Marx said that the most momentous thing happening in the world was the slave movement, on the one hand in America started by the death of John Brown the abolitionist, and in Russia on the other with the emancipation of the serfs. In the American Civil War, Marx and Engels were enthusiastic supporters of the North. Marx wrote many articles for the *New York Tribune*. (In fact Engels wrote many of them at first because Marx's English wasn't good enough, but later on he wrote them himself.) They also supported the right of the Polish to independence and they also were again huge enthusiasts for the Fenians and the Irish nationalist struggle. Marx was very critical of the Fenians when they blew up a prison in Clerkenwell, but he was very much in support of the Irish struggle. His youngest daughter called herself a Fenian and wore green. Both of Engels' relationships were with supporters of the Irish struggle - first with Mary Burns and then after her death with her sister Lizzie. Marx is always seen as a writer first and foremost - the first volume of *Capital* was finished in 1867 - but he was also very much immersed in real struggles.

It was this involvement which led him to help with the establishment of what became known as the First International (as opposed to the Second International set up by, among others, Marx's daughter in the late 1880s, and the Third International which was set up as a result of the Russian Revolution). The First International was founded as the International Workingmen's Association on 28 September 1864, from international organisations from France, Italy and Germany, but also from a section of people in Britain, which included Marx and a number of the trade union leaders, particularly from the building trade. Marx very quickly became the leading organising figure. He believed that the working class had to organise, and on an international basis. It was, I suppose, the equivalent of what we would now call a united front, a campaign which involved people with quite different political perspectives, where they came together over specific issues. Marx would write to Engels at various points about how he could not put issues in terms of revolution, but that the key was to get everyone organised and all fighting back.

Marx thought the victory of the American North in the Civil War gave an impetus to democracy in Europe. Then in 1870, there was a war between France and Germany (which was just unifying under Bismarck), which ended with the siege of Paris. Marx's middle daughter Laura was married to a Frenchman - indeed two of his daughters were married to Frenchmen - and was living in Paris when the siege happened. The outcome of the defeat of France in 1871 was then the establishment of the first workers' government - what was called the Paris Commune.

His daughter Jenny said that during the whole time of the Paris Commune, from March to the end of May 1871, Marx and Engels would go for long walks, worrying about what would happen. Politically they were worried because they wanted this democratic, workers' government to succeed, but they were also worried because they had so many family, friends and old comrades who were involved in the fighting. Some of their old friends were indeed killed, like their comrade Gustav Flourens whose body was thrown onto a dustcart. Just after the fall of the Commune, Laura and her husband had managed to get away from Paris and had gone to Bordeaux. Jenny and Eleanor, who was only 16, went to visit them. They were arrested and interrogated for many hours. Jenny had letters in her bag from Gustav Flourens and from an Irish nationalist, and had either of them been found, these two girls would have been deported to a penal colony. Marx's wife Jenny wrote, 'you can't have any idea of how much my husband, the girls and all of us have suffered because of the French events'.

Marx drew the conclusion from the bloody end of the

Commune that the working class cannot simply lay hold of a ready-made state machinery and wield it for their own purpose. He understood then that working-class power has to destroy the old state machinery if it is to be successful in creating a democratic revolution. This was extremely controversial and marked the effective end of the First International. However, Marx's *The Civil War in France* became very popular and made him even more of a well-known figure. London was full of exiles from the commune, one of whom, Lissagaray, became engaged to Eleanor. Marx very much disapproved of the engagement and it never led to marriage, but he knew and worked with the Communards for the rest of his life.

He had around another ten years of life, but he was increasingly ill. He suffered quite a few illnesses - he smoked very heavily - and his personal life was increasingly hard. He tried to finish the other two volumes of *Capital* but didn't succeed and they were finished after his death by Engels, among others, with help from Eleanor. He died in 1883, but not before he lost both his wife and his oldest daughter. His funeral was very small and in fact the Marx daughters never wanted a monument for him. A year after he died, many people joined the Commune anniversary demonstration as a commemoration of his life, and they saw this and his work was his legacy – a living revolutionary movement rather than a monument of stone. When he died, Engels said at the funeral that he was above all else a revolutionary, which was a true and fitting epitaph to his life.

2. Marx's Philosophy

Chris Nineham

Few if any intellectual figures have had as much impact on the world as Marx. And yet Marx's ideas are rarely taken seriously in education, in the media or in cultural life. In mainstream political discussions they are practically taboo.

It is worth considering why this is. One reason concerns the limits of contemporary philosophy. Marx sought to understand the world in all its interconnections: 'the whole thing can be depicted in its totality,'[1] he wrote. Today there is a widespread prejudice against big explanations or 'grand narratives'. Attempts at a holistic or total understanding of the world are routinely dismissed as 'merely ideological' or even dangerous. Trying to understand society as a totality, we are sometimes even told, is mysteriously liable to lead to totalitarianism.

As we shall see, ever since the Enlightenment, philosophers have had difficulties developing a coherent, unified worldview. But in recent decades, whole schools of philosophy have developed, dedicated to proving that big explanations are inherently wrong-headed. The tendency to see the world partially is deeply ingrained. You only have to turn on the TV news to witness an instinct to deal with different aspects of reality as separate and unconnected.

Similar attitudes permeate politics. Margaret Thatcher understood that intellectual resignation and political submission were connected. She took the denial of social reality to an endpoint when she announced 'there is no such thing as society', and the claim went hand in hand with her famous mantra 'there is no alternative'. Since then official thinking has pulled back from these outlying positions, but the idea that reality is too complex and fragmentary to be consciously controlled remains essential to the argument for a small state and laissez faire economics.

So Marx's original sin was to seek to understand society as an integrated system. He followed up with two other transgressions. First, he concluded that capitalist society is so deeply flawed, divided and oppressive, that it is unsustainable, not to say indefensible:

> *Modern Industry has converted the little workshop of the patriarchal master into the great factory of the industrial capitalist. Masses of labourers, crowded into the factory, are organised like soldiers. As privates of the industrial army they are placed under the command of a perfect hierarchy of officers and sergeants. Not only are they slaves of the bourgeois class, and of the bourgeois State; they are daily and hourly enslaved by the machine, by the overlooker, and, above all, by the individual bourgeois manufacturer himself. The more openly this despotism proclaims gain to be its end and aim, the more petty, the more hateful and the more embittering it is.*[2]

Second, he took the side of those who suffer and are oppressed in this divided world. Whereas establishment ideologues tend to overlook or conceal the interests implicit in their philosophical views, Marxism is openly partisan. For Marx, to attempt neutrality in the context of a polarised and unequal society is to take sides, to defend the status quo. He went further and concluded that society can only be properly understood from the point of view of the exploited.

If Marxism is partisan, it is also active. Marx's famous phrase 'philosophers have interpreted the world in various ways, the point is to change it',[3] is written on his gravestone. It can be misconstrued. He didn't mean by it that interpreting the world is unimportant or that we should abandon philosophy in favour of positivistic science. He meant something more complex - that interpreting the world should not be divorced from the active attempt to change it. If it is, not only is knowledge reduced to mere contemplation and practical irrelevance, but understanding itself will be compromised. At the heart of Marx's philosophy is the idea that humans can only have access to an understanding of the world when we are in the process of acting on it:

> *The question whether objective truth can be attributed to human thinking is not a question of theory but is a practical question. Man must prove the truth - i.e. the reality and power, the this-sidedness of his thinking in practice. The dispute over the reality or non-reality of thinking that is isolated from practice is a purely scholastic question.*[4]

The limits of the Enlightenment

Marx's crucial intellectual breakthroughs took place in the early 1840s. The political and philosophical life of these years was still shaped by the complex legacy of the French Revolution of 1789. That revolution, adopting many of the ideas of the rationalist Enlightenment philosophers, had written on its banner the principles of liberty, fraternity and equality. But it was clear by the early years of the nineteenth century that it had failed to deliver them. Napoleon, the last embodiment of the revolution, had crowned himself Emperor in 1804 and was in any case militarily defeated in 1815. Monarchy and reaction had been re-imposed around Europe. This wasn't a simple restoration. The revolution had helped unleash the new forces of capitalism and the balance of class forces in society was changing fast, but political liberation seemed as far away as ever.

The question for progressives remained: how could

the promises and ideals of the revolution be made reality? The answer depended partly on how you conceived the relationship between humans and the social and natural worlds. Enlightenment philosophy had begun to clear away the mysticism and fatalism that had dominated the old world of the feudal hierarchies. It had unseated divine providence in theory. But it hadn't found a satisfactory new way to conceive of humanity's role. Philosophers had tended to be divided into those who stressed the power of ideas in making history and those who emphasised the way we are shaped by our environment, by the external world. Both 'idealists' and 'materialists' had come up against the limits of their method.

Hegel, the greatest of the idealists, who had a profound influence on Marx, went as far as conceiving of history itself as the unfolding of the human spirit, or the 'absolute idea.' The result was that in his work he tended to try to remould reality to fit his concepts. In Marx's words, he engaged in 'the philosophical dissolution and restoration of the empirical world.'[5] On the other hand, the materialists, who started with the outside world, had problems theorising any active role for consciousness at all. For them, reality simply imprinted itself on our senses. Neither idealists nor materialists had managed to explain how consciousness and the material world interrelated.

Standing philosophy on its head

Marx's first move in overcoming this problem was the apparently simple one of placing humans back into the material world, of understanding human beings 'as they really are':

> We do not set out from what men say, imagine, conceive, nor from men as narrated, thought of, imagined, conceived, in order to arrive at men in the flesh. We set out from real, active men, and on the basis of their real life-process we demonstrate the

development of the ideological reflexes and echoes of this life-process.[6]

The idealist procedure of interpreting social reality through the notions that people have about themselves remains standard in history to this day. But for Marx, ideas were the wrong starting point: 'it is not consciousness of men that determines their being, but, on the contrary, their social being that determines their consciousness.'[7]

He saw that all aspects of human existence, including politics, art and culture, the sorts of relationships we have and so forth, are shaped by the kind of society we live in and particularly by its 'life processes', the way the rudiments of survival are organised.

At the same time as overcoming idealism by conceiving human societies as material processes, Marx was also moving beyond the passive, contemplative stance of 'mechanical' materialism. In *The German Ideology*, the first rounded exposition of their method, Marx and his collaborator Engels reintroduced history, change and activity into materialist thought:

> *Morality, religion, metaphysics, all the rest of ideology and their corresponding forms of consciousness, thus no longer retain the semblance of independence. They have no history, no development; but men, developing their material production and their material intercourse, alter, along with this their real existence, their thinking and the products of their thinking.*[8]

Throughout the rest of his life, Marx developed the immense explanatory power of what came to be called historical materialism. It allowed him to grasp the laws of motion of successive forms of economic organisation and trace their impact on social life. Famously, in *The Communist Manifesto*, he explored the extraordinary transformation unleashed by capitalist development:

> *The bourgeoisie, wherever it has got the upper hand, has put an end to all feudal, patriarchal, idyllic relations. It has pitilessly torn asunder the motley feudal ties that bound man to his "natural superiors", and has left remaining no other nexus between man and man than naked self-interest, than callous "cash payment". It has drowned the most heavenly ecstasies of religious fervour, of chivalrous enthusiasm, of philistine sentimentalism, in the icy water of egotistical calculation. … The bourgeoisie cannot exist without constantly revolutionising the instruments of production, and thereby the relations of production, and with them the whole relations of society… All fixed, fast-frozen relations, with their train of ancient and venerable prejudices and opinions, are swept away, all new-formed ones become antiquated before they can ossify. All that is solid melts into air, all that is holy is profaned, and man is at last compelled to face with sober senses his real conditions of life, and his relations with his kind.*[9]

Marx's method is sometimes mistakenly accused of reductionism. But in asserting the primacy of economics in the social life and development of class societies, he was quite specifically *not* trying to collapse all orders of reality into the realm of economics. For him, different levels of reality formed interconnected aspects of a contradictory whole, and seeking the material roots of things provided unparalleled insight into the concealed significance of all kinds of social phenomena. Debates about religion, for example, were central in the development of Marx's ideas, and his discussion of the subject remains strikingly relevant today. Religion, Marx insisted, was not just a mistaken set of ideas that could be eradicated by rational argument. Its real meaning, and its survival into the modern world, could only be understood by grasping its material, and therefore its psychological, sources. More than anything, religion was a reaction to the misery and lack of control people experience in class society:

> *Religious suffering is, at one and the same time, the expression of real suffering and a protest against real suffering. Religion is the sigh of the oppressed creature, the heart of a heartless world, and the soul of soulless conditions, the opium of the people.*[10]

Here, Marx was providing the key to understanding apparently perplexing behaviour, but this in no way implied that he thought religion was unimportant. Far from it. He was pointing out the material basis of religion precisely because he knew how much of an influence it continued to have. But in the process, he was also pointing to the action necessary to overcome it. The apparitions of religion, he argued, could only be laid to rest by abolishing the conditions that gave rise to them, 'after the earthly family is discovered to be the secret of the holy family, the former must then be destroyed in theory and in practice'.[11]

Marx's pathbreaking conception of human society as a material process changing over time was subversive at a whole number of levels. By focusing on the different ways societies had been organised historically, he suggested that the current reality was temporary. By showing how different economic regimes had thrown up different moral codes and values, he challenged the philosophers' tendency to invent timeless abstractions about human nature.

Most important of all, emphasising the role of economic organisation in structuring society suggested the necessity of much more far reaching change than most radicals had considered up to this point. For the whole of bourgeois philosophy at the time saw politics as a function of the state. It was axiomatic that the state had a necessary role as manager of the natural antagonisms in civil society. Change could only come about from above by modifying political life. Marx turned this view on its head. For Marx, the state was an expression of a fundamentally divided society, and its ultimate role was to maintain those divisions in the interests of the rulers. Thus not only was the state's oppressive role unnecessary, but the secret to dispensing with it was to reorganise society from the ground up.

Piecemeal change to the superstructure - changing laws, making partial reforms, even changing governments, however important these things were - would not therefore fundamentally transform our lives. If we want a qualitatively different society, then we need both to confront the state and overturn the deep structures that form the basis of society. We need not just political, but social revolution.

Marx's approach also identified processes which might make such change possible. Over time, he argued, economic development within particular social structures creates tensions in society as 'the material forces of production enter into contradiction with the existing relations of production.' The internal development of capitalism, for example, leads to the development of a class that is capable of surpassing it:

> *Hand in hand with this centralisation, or this expropriation of many capitalists by few, develop, on an ever-extending scale, the cooperative form of the labour process, the conscious technical application of science, the methodical cultivation of the soil, the transformation of the instruments of labour into instruments of labour only usable in common, the economizing of all means of production by their use as means of production of combined, socialized labour, the entanglement of all peoples in the net of the world market, and with this, the international character*

of the capitalistic regime. Along with the constantly diminishing number of the magnates of capital, who usurp and monopolize all advantages of this process of transformation, grows the mass of misery, oppression, slavery, degradation, exploitation; but with this too grows the revolt of the working class, a class always increasing in numbers, and disciplined, united, organized by the very mechanism of the process of capitalist production itself.[12]

Labour and the chance of freedom

Marx is often dismissed as a crude determinist, someone who believed that change is the inevitable outcome of impersonal historical developments. This is a complete distortion. In fact, supporters of the free market – often the people who condemn Marx on this count – are much more vulnerable than Marxists to this criticism. The neoliberals' cry, 'let the market decide' is precisely asking us to abandon human agency and put all our trust in the vagaries of an economic system.

In fact, what is probably most irritating to establishment ideologues is that Marx believed it was possible to escape the world of necessity and move beyond a rhetorical commitment to personal freedom. The whole of his work was dedicated to finding the way to a society which would allow the 'all round development of individuals.'[13] What is more, for Marx this could only happen when humanity had managed to consciously control the whole process of social production:

Freedom in this field (of labour) can only consist in socialized man, the associated producers, rationally regulating their interchange with Nature; and achieving this with the least expenditure of energy and under conditions most favourable to, and worthy of, their human nature.[14]

The optimism on display here was based on Marx's assessment of human beings' unique capacities. Learning from Hegel and the British political economists, Marx saw human existence as based on labour - human beings' ability, in fact our need, to consciously and collectively work on the world in order to change it. For Marx it is this characteristic, this restless propensity to transform the world, that defines humanity. It is this that gives us our ability to exponentially increase the wealth and resources available to us. But innovation is also implicit in labour. And every technical innovation impacts on our relations with each other, challenging how we organise socially. The ability to consciously labour contains within it the potential to plan and change the kind of society we live in. In the meantime, it gives us the capacity to imagine how things could be different:

> *A spider conducts operations that resemble those of a weaver, and a bee puts to shame many an architect in the construction of her cells. But what distinguishes the worst architect from the best of bees is this, that the architect raises his structure in imagination before he erects it in reality.*[15]

If humans have this ability to adapt and construct our social world, the question then arises, why hasn't positive change happened? Why do we still live in such a profoundly unequal and dysfunctional society? The answer, Marx says, lies in the structure of the society we have inherited and the dead weight of the past:

> *Men make their own history, but they do not make it as they please; they do not make it under self-selected circumstances, but under circumstances existing already, given and transmitted from the past. The tradition of all dead generations weighs like a nightmare on the brains of the living.*[16]

The political structures of class societies are designed to block change. The great bourgeois revolutions might have dismantled the hierarchies of feudalism, but for all their great advances they created new tyrannies. The exploding levels of wealth produced by emerging capitalism made the satisfaction of human needs a possibility for the first time in history. But that wealth was concentrated in the hands of a new ruling class. From their strongholds in industry, the capitalists adapted the state edifice to secure their rule involving class-based law, a loyal civil service, a repressive police force, a servile press and so on. All this worked to ensure, amongst other things, that the ideas of the ruling class dominated society. As Marx drily commented, 'the class which has the means of material production at its disposal, has control at the same time over the means of mental production'.[17]

Class and alienation

But there is also a deeper process inhibiting change. Under capitalism, labour - the true expression of our nature and the secret to our creative capacities - is turned more completely than ever into its opposite. The new ruling class disciplines labour for its own ends and exploits it in a hi-tech, high productivity modern-day slavery based on the alienation of other peoples' labour power.

This has a double-sided effect. On the one hand, by squeezing previously unimagineable levels of wealth from labour, capitalism immiserates the vast majority of the population and creates its nemesis, what Marx called its gravedigger. By so comprehensively robbing the majority not just of any serious share in property, but even of its labour power, capitalism has created a class that has no stake in the survival of the system. Workers in fact have a direct interest in the abolition of the system, and certainly no interest in oppressing any other section of society. This is what Marx meant when he called the working class the first universal class, a class with 'radical chains'.[18] Not only do workers have the potential power to change society because of their strategic location as the real creators of wealth, but they have access to a unique perspective because their only prospect of freedom comes with the complete transformation of society:

> *All previous historical movements were movements of minorities, or in the interest of minorities. The proletarian movement is the self-conscious, independent movement of the immense majority, in the interest of the immense majority. The proletariat, the lowest stratum of our present society, cannot stir, cannot raise itself up, without the whole superincumbent strata of official society being sprung into the air.*[19]

But at the very same time, the alienation of labour has a profoundly debilitating effect. It robs us of control over our labour power and any influence over the way production is organised, what is produced, who it is produced for and so forth. This impacts very deeply on us, as Marx explained in the poetic language of the *Economic and Philosophic Manuscripts of 1844*:

> *The more the worker exerts himself in his work, the more powerful the alien, objective world becomes which he brings into being against himself, the poorer he and his inner world become, and the less they belong to him... In his work, therefore, he does not affirm himself but denies himself, does not feel content but unhappy, does not develop freely his physical and mental energy but mortifies his body and ruins his mind. The worker therefore only feels himself outside his work, and in his work feels outside himself. He feels at home when he is not working, and when he is working he does not feel at home.*[20]

Because production mediates our relationships with nature and with each other, the fact that we are alienated in the process of production distorts our connections with nature and with other human beings. Because the process of labour is so central to our humanity, we are in fact alienated from our own abilities.

Furthermore, capitalist production turns our labour power into a commodity to be bought and sold like any other. We are partially products of capitalism ourselves:

> *Production does not simply produce man as a commodity... it produces him in keeping with this role as a spiritually and physically dehumanised being. – Immorality, deformity, and dullness of the workers and the capitalists. – Its product is the self-conscious and self-acting commodity... The commodity-man.*[21]

This distortion of workers' essential being - their ability to produce collectively and consciously - in the routine of commodity production and privatised survival, can deeply effect their understanding of the situation. Collective interests can be obscured, leaving only a sense of powerlessness and atomisation. This opens up the possibility that workers can internalise the ideas and values of those who rule over them.

The necessary revolution

Marx, then, had identified a series of contradictions at the heart of capitalist society. Firstly, he perceived the contradiction between human beings' creative potential and the way labour, and therefore society more generally, is organised. Secondly, he grasped that exploitation produces a real-world struggle, 'now hidden, now open', between the two main classes, the workers and the capitalists. Periodically, the sharp divergence of interests between working people and the capitalist class breaks out into open conflict, in the form of demonstrations, riots, strikes or, at times of acute crisis, revolutionary movements.

The result he saw, in turn, is the existence of deeply contradictory ideas in people's minds, expressing both sides of this reality. People can simultaneously show solidarity for other members of their class *and* accept at least some of the backward ideas promoted in the mainstream. People can support increasing taxes for the rich but also believe that we should stop immigration or get tough with welfare scroungers.

How do these contradictions play out? The notion of a contradictory unity was central to Marx's dialectical understanding the world. Existing antagonisms could only be overcome through a confrontation that would transform the whole. The outcome of this struggle depends on many things - the level of social development, the balance of forces between different classes and groups, the prevailing ideas in society and so forth. But it is not fixed in advance. It depends also on conscious human intervention.

Typically for Marx, the resolution to these connected contradictions, including the contradictions in consciousness, was a practical matter. It lay in action and organisation. We have seen that Marx argued that revolution is a necessary condition for far-reaching change because the capitalist system is so deeply entrenched, and because inequality and injustice is written into its very DNA. But there are other reasons why revolutionary activity is important. For Marx, it is only such activity that can tilt the balance in favour of a critical understanding of society and a recovery of human capacities. If it is true that capitalism, as well as creating opposition and resistance, can demoralise and atomise, the solution is increasing the level of activism and participation in mass movements and developing intellectual clarity in the process. It is in the process of changing the world, Marx argues, that people change themselves. Part One of *The German Ideology* ends with a call to arms:

Both for the production on a mass scale of this communist consciousness, and for the success of the cause itself, the alteration of men on a mass scale is necessary, an alteration which can only take place in a practical movement, a revolution; this revolution is necessary, therefore, not only because the ruling class cannot be overthrown in any other way, but also because the class overthrowing it can only in a revolution succeed in ridding itself of all the muck of ages and become fitted to found society anew.[22]

It is worth noting two things here. First, the deeply democratic spirit of this argument. Seeing the self-activity of working people - the majority of society - is the key to change is infinitely more democratic than the notion of choosing between a small number of candidates with very similar ideas once every five years to govern over us.

The second thing is that it implies conscious action and organisation. It is in the realm of strategy and action that understanding that Marx was definitively *not* a determinist is most important. For him, change wasn't inevitable, nor is it inevitable that people fully understand the world they live in. Both depended on human activity and, linked to it, the conscious development of organisations with coherent strategies and ideas. Without such conscious, organised activity, class struggle could end in the 'common ruin of the contending classes' rather than successful revolution.

Once again today, it is becoming clear to millions of people that capitalism offers little prospect of taking humanity forward. The system is wracked by a series of crises that threaten the very future of whole societies. It is also clear that the experience of living in this society can both radicalise and demoralise, that it can unleash both forces of progress and forces of despair.

In general people become open to radical ideas, to a politics of hope, through activity, through being involved in struggle and campaigning. But those struggles need to be organised, and the connections need to be clearly made between today's immediate struggles and the potential for the wholesale re-organisation of society. Those of us who aspire to radical change have then a responsibility to organise together to take that struggle forward on the widest possible basis and try and to convince others of our collective transformative power. This is the core of Marx's philosophy of action.

Notes

1. Marx and Engels (1989) *The German Ideology*, London: Lawrence and Wishart, p.58.
2. Marx and Engels (1983) *The Communist Manifesto*, London: Lawrence and Wishart, p.14.
3. Marx and Engels (1989) Theses on Feuerbach, in *The German Ideology*, p.121.
4. Ibid, p.121.
5. Marx (1977) Economic and Philosophical Manuscripts, in *Early Writings*, London: Penguin, p.384.
6. Marx and Engels (1989) *The German Ideology*, London: Lawrence and Wishart, p.47.
7. Marx (1977) Preface to A Contribution to the Critique of Political Economy, in *Early Writings*, p.425.
8. Ibid, p.47.
9. Marx and Engels (1983) *The Communist Manifesto*, London: Lawrence and Wishart, p.16.
10. Marx (1977) A Contribution to the Critique of Hegel's Philosophy of Right, in *Early Writings*, p.244.
11. Marx and Engels (1989) Theses on Feuerbach, in *The German Ideology*, p.22.
12. Marx (1976) *Capital*, Volume 1, London: Penguin, p.929.
13. Marx and Engels (1989) Theses on Feuerbach, in *The German Ideology*, p.117.
14. Marx (1991) *Capital*, Volume 3, London: Penguin, p.959.
15. Ibid, p.253.
16. Marx, (1987) *The Eighteenth Brumaire of Louis Bonaparte*, London: Lawrence and Wishart, p.10.
17. Marx and Engels (1989) Theses on Feuerbach, in *The German Ideology*, p.64.
18. Marx, (1977) A Contribution to the Critique of Hegel's Philosophy of Right, in *Early Writings*, p.256.
19. Marx and Engels (1983) *The Communist Manifesto*, London: Lawrence and Wishart, p.19.

20. Marx (1977) Economic and Philosophical Manuscripts in *Early Writings*, London: Penguin, pp.324-326.
21. Ibid, p.338.
22. Marx and Engels (1989) *The German Ideology*, London: Lawrence and Wishart, p.95.

3. Marx's Economics

James Meadway

Karl Marx begins his analysis of capitalism in the most obvious, easiest place to start: with money. It's very hard to imagine a capitalism without money and, as Marx explores the implications of using money in the first few chapters of *Capital*, its centrality to the whole system is made clear.

Marx calls this method 'rising from the abstract to the concrete'. The system is hugely complex. But by starting with the simplest elements of the system, we can begin to piece together the whole. However, at the same time, we need to start with a simple element that provides a route to understanding the system in its entirety. We can't just look at simple parts in isolation from their place in the whole, because the way the system behaves is different from merely adding up all of its separate elements. The whole is greater than (and different from) the sum of its parts.

The further complexity here is that, unlike the natural sciences, a social science is studying something in which we are all implicated: human society. We can't separate ourselves from that society, and we can't try and understand that society without also knowing that we are part of it, and helping to shape it on the basis of our ideas.

This has two direct results. First, no fact in economics arrives without being attached to some theory, since to construct empirical evidence requires us to have a theoretical understanding of what we wish to measure or analyse. Second, to understand the system we have also to understand different theories of the system, because different theoretical understandings of the system themselves help shape it. It is for this reason that Marx subtitled *Capital* a 'critique of political economy'. As well as being a guide to capitalism, it is a criticism of existing economics.

Commodities and money

So, to begin our analysis, we must find a part of the system that is both as simple as possible and, at the same time, central to the functioning of the system as a whole. Marx therefore begins with something without which it is impossible to imagine capitalism existing: money, and, with money, the commodity.

A commodity is anything that can be bought and sold for money. Marx labels capitalism a system of 'generalised commodity production'. In other words, this principle of exchanges for money is the dominant means, unlike all previous societies, in which the products of that society (be they cars or haircuts) are distributed. Marx notes, however, that in order to be exchanged, a commodity must be wanted or needed by someone: he calls this property the commodity's use-value. Its use-value is the unique property of a commodity that makes it wanted or needed. It is a distinct quality of the commodity, and as such it cannot be substituted directly by some other commodity. It is no good (to continue the example) getting a car when you need a haircut.

However, these commodities exchange, and they exchange in an orderly fashion. This is the flipside of every commodity: alongside its unique use-value, it holds an exchange-value. This exchange-value is not unique; it is a relationship of this commodity, with its unique use-value, to every other commodity, with their own use-values. It describes how many of this particular commodity would need to be offered in exchange for another. Every commodity in existence is a combination of a specific use-value and a general exchange-value.

Now, the complication here should be immediately obvious. We do not exchange commodities directly for each other. We use money. It is money that enables exchanges to take place. We buy and we sell with money. It functions as a standard of comparison that makes exchange possible. Marx calls money, on this basis, the 'universal equivalent': it allows exchange-values to be expressed, and therefore allows perhaps radically different commodities to be exchanged for each other. (We will look, later on, at how those different exchange-values are established.) The whole economy looks like a system of exchanges, with money as the essential element that allows these exchanges to take place.

The circulation of commodities

'Money makes the world go round,' as the film *Cabaret* has it. In particular, money, passing from hand to hand as people buy and sell, makes commodities move. As the money moves from those seeking to buy to those looking to sell, commodities move in the other direction. The commodities are what we value, of course: as above, commodities have an exchange-value only because they also have a use-value.

Money, from this point of view, has the purpose only of obtaining for us other use-values. And if we put all these circuits of money (passing from buyer to seller) and commodities (passing from seller to buyer) together, we can start to see the economy as the endless circulation of commodities in exchange. I sell a commodity to obtain money and, using this money, I buy another commodity. Everyone else does the same. Assuming labour, our ability to work, is a commodity, this seems to make sense. Marx described this process using a very simple notation:

$$C-M-C'$$

C is the commodity. M is money. C' is a different commodity. C-M is the process of sale, swapping a commodity for cash. And M-C' is the process of purchase, swapping cash for a commodity. The start and end of the process are commodities, obtained to meet real human needs and wants. Money appears to be simply a convenient means by which the exchange of commodities can take place. Likewise, the exchanges all seem reasonable: if no compulsion is introduced, and markets are allowed to operate freely, commodities will exchange for the appropriate amounts of money, equal to their value, and vice versa. Capitalism is a fair system – or so it seems.

If you've studied mainstream economics at all, generally labelled 'neoclassical' economics, this will be a familiar story. Money is a mere cipher; the economy exists to satisfy human needs, with money appearing only because continually bartering one commodity for another is too fiddly and time-consuming. It is wants that power the economy along and, with a small amount of maths, it can be 'proved' that a market-based economy is the most efficient means to ensure a distribution of commodities that best matches those wants, given available resources.

There is a problem with this benign view of capitalism. First, where do crises come from? If commodities are simply swapping for other commodities, how can it be the case that piles of unsold goods can appear in a recession? Why would the circulation of commodities break down in this way? (One venerable result in mainstream economics, known as Say's Law, holds that it can't.)

Second, why should this nice flow of commodities, facilitated by money, lead to outcomes in which some of those taking part in the circulation are made progressively richer – and others are not? If everything is being exchanged on the basis of the equality, with a commodity worth £10 exchanging for £10 (or whatever amount it is), it should not be possible for (as it seems) someone persistently to generate more money from the process.

Money making money, and the drive to compete

It is in answering these two questions that Marx presents his most radical critique of mainstream economics.

Capitalism is not a system designed to meet human needs and desires. It arose, instead, on the basis of a simple principle: that money can produce more money. Capitalism's major institutions, from the stock market to businesses, are structured around this simple principle. Its history is the history of the application of this principle: from the merchants of medieval Italy, trading the goods of the Far East, to a global corporation like BP, the history of capitalism is the history of this accumulation.

Marx calls money that can become more money 'capital'. It is because capital exists that money must create more money. Capital expands over time: money becomes more money. And the economy capital exists in, capitalism, has special structures intended to compel money to create more money. Principal amongst these is the role of competition. Capital does not exist as a single entity. The economy contains many, many firms (and states). Capital exists only as many different capitals, and each unit of capital is locked into merciless competition with every other. Sometimes this competition can be hidden. Sometimes it can even be organised, temporarily, out of existence, as when firms create cartels – groups of firms agreeing on certain objectives. More often, the state, as a regulator of this competition, can attempt to restrain it – for example, in laws protecting the environment. But competition reappears, compelling the accumulation of greater and greater amounts of capital. And the drive to accumulate batters continually against restraint placed upon it. 'Accumulate, accumulate!' wrote Marx of capitalism's internal drive. 'That is Moses and the prophets.'

Firms are the typical way in which capital is organised in most capitalist societies today, including Britain. They are locked into merciless competition, particularly when they sell similar commodities. The sanctions on a firm that fails to compete effectively, and so does not accumulate rapidly enough, are harsh: it becomes bankrupt, and ceases to exist. Sainsbury's is competing with Tesco is competing with Aldi. But behind the firms, away from the markets for the commodities they sell, competition is ferocious amongst those who own the capital – the capitalists. The institutions through which investment in capital is managed and organised are generally referred to as the financial markets. Finance can take many different forms, from shares on a stock market, to corporate bonds (loans made to companies), to venture capital (private investment). But in each case the logic of the market and the structures of the institutions demand a certain pace of accumulation. The return on capital is enforced by the market, and firms consistently failing to produce this return will go bankrupt.

This is the world of competition, and of money generating more money, that we actually inhabit. It has nothing to do with answering human needs and wants: it is not organised around the production of use-values, but of exchange-values. A commodity will need to have some use-value for it to be sold at all. But in a world of competing capital, it is the exchange-value that is being sought.

The true situation is the complete inverse of the mainstream story. Marx showed the inversion in this notation:

M-C-M'

Money is exchanged for a commodity (M-C). This commodity is then exchanged for a different and (ideally) greater sum of money (C-M'). This is perhaps the single most important statement in all of Marx's voluminous economic writings. It is the core of capitalism, and it is utterly ruthless in its consequences. Human needs and wants are incidental to the monstrous drive to continually accumulate greater and greater sums of money.

'The hidden abode of production'
Capitalists are vicious amongst themselves. They

compete. They scheme and plot and attempt desperately to outmanoeuvre one another. The price of failure is the destruction of their precious capital. Yet this merciless competition, reducing all calculations to the necessity of profit, can be presented as a good thing. The economist Joseph Schumpeter, a firm believer in capitalism, influentially argued that it was the disruption and chaos of this competition that gave capitalism its immense dynamism. 'Creative destruction' was enforced - capitalists seeking new ways to innovate and provide new products and services. This drive to accumulate had created a new, dynamic world of continual innovation. In less sophisticated and more ideological form, this vision of capitalism is ubiquitous today. Think of the praise heaped on Apple's Steve Jobs, for instance, or television programmes like *The Apprentice* or *Dragon's Den*.

Marx, for his part, certainly recognised the dynamism. *The Communist Manifesto* praises, at some length, the way in which capitalism has, during its short history, created 'more massive and more colossal productive forces than have all preceding generations together.' This dynamism arrives at a price, however. To see the costs of capitalist dynamism, we need to step outside of the land of free exchange, 'a very Eden of the innate rights of man' (Marx sarcastically writes) and into 'the hidden abode of production'.

It is here that the secret of money producing money is revealed. Nothing to do with the magic of the financial sector: Marx locates the dynamism of capitalism as opposed to the circuit of money itself, since it is only by acquiring money and turning it into commodities that production can begin. As we have seen, at least in theory anything can become a commodity once it has been offered for sale. The aim of capitalist production is only to produce commodities so as to allow money invested to produce money returns. So 'production' here may well extend to the production of commodities far removed from factories and manufacturing. Hairdressing is produced under capitalism; likewise, most of the roughly 70% of the British economy tied up in services is productive in this sense of producing commodities.

Marx illustrated the process by expanding his earlier shorthand:

$$M\text{-}C...P...C'\text{-}M'$$

Here, we see that a middle term, P, has been introduced between the M-M' money cycle. But notice also that this production process has split up the commodity: we now have C being turned, through production, into different commodities, C'.

This goes to the heart of the matter. Production transforms the world, and by transforming the world, allows money to become more money. Under capitalism, this process has become systematic. Money is advanced, commodities are bought, production happens - and then, when the new commodities are sold, more money is returned. Profits are made like this.

But if the process is systematic, there must be some institution in capitalism that enables it to occur. Production does not haphazardly produce profits. It does it systematically. As the circuits of money and commodities whirl round and round, those holding capital use it, ultimately, to buy commodities that enable production to occur. The institution that enables this systematic production of profits to take place is the labour market.

It is here that we get to the centre not just of Marx's theory of capitalism, but his theory of history. At the centre of this theory is labour - by which Marx means the ability of humans to think about and transform the world they live in. How labour is organised, and who organises it, is critical to Marx's understanding of how history changes.

Under capitalism, labour, like everything else, becomes a commodity. It is bought and sold on the labour market.

However, those who sell their labour are not slaves: they are free individuals entering into free contracts with those buying their labour. Individuals are not bought and sold, but individuals' capacity to work is. It is this distinction that gives Marx the means to show how profits can be systematically produced. Labour requires some payments to reproduce itself. Workers must be paid enough to ensure they are fit, healthy and able to work - plus, over time, some 'moral or historical' element reflecting accepted (and hard-won) minimum standards.

The *capacity* to work, however, is something distinct from this: whilst the capitalist needs to pay the worker to ensure they are able and willing to come to work, once they are at work, their capacity to work can be used as the capitalist directs. By managing this capacity to work, the capitalist can transform the inputs into production - whatever they may be - into different outputs, which they can sell. But since they pay that labourer only the value necessary to secure their time at work, the value of what the labourer produces can vary from this. In particular, it can be more than the value it costs to buy the labourer's time.

This is Marx's theory of exploitation. Workers produce more value at work than it costs to employ them. Note that Marx is using 'exploitation' in a different sense to the one we are used to: a very well-paid worker, for example an engineer or train driver, can still be exploited in this sense since they are producing more value for the capitalist employing them than they are being paid for. In other words, the use-value of labour is the capacity to work: to think about and transform the world. The exchange-value of labour is quite different: it is the cost of reproducing that labourer, ensuring he or she can turn up for work again.

By systematically organising production in this way, through the labour market, the capitalists as a class can hope to systematically produce profits - or, to use Marx's terminology, 'surplus value'. Marx has a labour theory of value: it is labour as such, 'socially necessary labour time', that sets the fundamental value of commodities being produced. Note, too, that it is only 'socially necessary labour time' that sets the value: the market generally determines this, setting the standard for efficient production. A capitalist doesn't earn more money by allowing his or her workers longer to produce: when it comes to sales, they will have higher costs than their competitors and so lose out, potentially going bankrupt. It is by this means that socially necessary labour time is enforced

This is not, however, labour floating freely of the world it inhabits. Marx strongly attacked those who argued that labour is the source of all value in his *Critique of the Gotha Programme*. It is labour working on the world that is a source of value: in other words, nature is just as much a source of value as human labour. We can see this very directly in the appalling environmental consequences of capitalism, with the money-producing-money process forcing the extraction of value from the environment.

It should be clear how useful unemployment is to the capitalist here. By raising the spectre of unemployment, capitalists in general can discipline their workers, holding down the price demanded for their labour. The 'reserve army of labour' (as Marx described the unemployed) marches beside all those employed and exploited directly. Both employed and unemployed have an incentive to remove the system of exploitation - but under capitalism their class interests can be turned against each other, in much the same way that migrant labour is used, or forms of oppression like racism and sexism function in relation to work. Divide and rule is the order of the day.

Growth and crisis
This turns conventional theories of the economy on their head. Far from being a system that produces growth over time, creating work, capitalism produces work that produces growth. The proceeds of this growth are

inherently shared unequally, due to the way power is structured inside society. It is not the case, as Schumpeter argued, that capitalists are innovators who shake up society with their innovations, producing growth: rather, capitalists take the proceeds of growth, derived from exploitation, and are compelled to innovate to defend that growth. Put another way, Steve Jobs may well have been a great innovator, but he was nothing without the exploitation that producing iPhones necessarily entails.

The system is complex. In theory, all this should hang together through the two circuits of money and commodities. But precisely because it is organised through money, dependent on competition and, finally, a society based on class, capitalism falls into crisis.

At the most abstract level, it is the presence of money that creates the possibility of the crisis. This is because money separates the act of selling from the act of buying; or rather, it imposes a distinction between the offer of a commodity for sale, and the desire of anyone to buy that commodity. This gives huge flexibility to the system, but creates the obvious problem that not all commodities offered for sale will necessarily also be bought. (This is Marx's fundamental critique of Say's Law.)

The breakdown here is merely theoretical, however. It opens the possibility of a crisis. What makes a crisis happen falls, fundamentally, into two parts: one on the side of the capitalist, the other on the side of the worker.

For the capitalist, dragged continually back to expand their holdings of money, profits are everything. Profits guarantee that money can produce more money over time and, as those profits are produced, they will be reinvested. But in the absence of profits, capitalists fall into crisis. If one individual capitalist fails to make a profit, that is bad for them. If capitalists in general fail to make profits, it is bad for the system as a whole. Capitalists can lose out on profits in two ways: the first, generally less likely, is that workers can use their labour power to extract a greater share of the surplus in their direction. The institution of unemployment generally ensures this cannot happen, although we can argue that something like this occurred during the period of 'full employment' of the post-war years, when powerful trade unions were able (directly or indirectly) to ensure rising real wages for most workers. What followed this squeeze on profits was the dramatic reassertion of class power in the form of Thatcherism and mass unemployment, declawing the trade union movement.

The second, arguably more fundamental problem, is with capitalist accumulation itself. As capitalists expand their businesses, they chase greater and greater profits through installing more and more machinery and equipment. New technology and new machinery enables them to steal a march on their rivals, grabbing markets and generating higher profits. But as capitalists enthusiastically try and steal one over their rivals, they are collectively swinging their investment away from the source of profits, exploited labour, and towards machinery. Over time, then, there is a pressure of the rate of profit - the amount of profit generated per pound invested - to fall. Marx called this the tendency of the rate of profit to fall, and it has been a source of controversy ever since he first suggested it, with economists disagreeing on its importance.

There are certainly 'countervailing tendencies'. The first is the capacity of new machinery to cheapen investment over time: as production becomes more efficient, profits can be restored. The second critical tendency is for capitalists to be able to squeeze labour, reducing pay, increasing hours and so restoring profits. This is crude but can be effective. One way to think about austerity, with its years of falling wages, is as an example of precisely this - profits have reached record highs in the UK in recent years.

But this route out of the crisis opens up a second route into a crisis. To obtain their profits, capitalists must sell their goods. Marx called this 'realising' their profits, with the unsold goods containing potential profits that had not yet been realised. But if everyone's pay is being squeezed to restore profits - who will buy all the commodities being produced? Marx called a crisis of this kind a 'realisation crisis'.

Capitalism, then, walks an unsteady path between two forms of crisis. Attempts to generate more profits, through investment or thorough wage cuts, lead into the crisis of realisation. Attempts to drive up wages, creating markets for commodities, will eventually eat into profits, bringing fresh crisis. In other words, nether austerity nor 'Keynesianism' can really solve the crisis. Capitalism wanders continually between the two, helping generate the powerful boom-bust pattern of the business cycle.

There is one means to break this process, within capitalism: allow the crisis to destroy capital. As firms go bankrupt, other firms can seize their markets and buy up their assets on the cheap. This enables those firms to restore their own profitability, ending the general crisis. Capitalism therefore has a self-regulating mechanism: eventually, it will crash so much that profits are boosted for the survivors and accumulation can begin again.

The state and finance

Two institutions, closely related to each other, have developed to ensure the process continues. The first is the state, which clearly pre-exists capitalism - indeed it exists in any class society - but adopts particular roles under capitalism. The second is finance, which, again, pre-dates capitalism proper, but which also occupies a particular place in capitalism.

Both are fundamentally concerned with resolving the three contradictions we have seen here: the competition between capitalists; the exploitation of workers by capitalists; and the cycle of profits and investment. They have developed these roles in haphazard, unplanned fashion, but today the two form amongst the most important parts of the capitalist economy.

States, in economic terms, provide laws and regulations to capitalism that allow (at least at the national level) some restraint in the competitive process. Over time, they have developed a number of roles particularly concerned with the reproduction of capitalism: providing education and healthcare, for example. And they can also directly intervene, to support individual capitals facing difficulties, or more generally in the provision of goods and services that individual capitals are unwilling or unable to provide - transport and utilities being the most obvious here. The state can act, to some extent, autonomously from private capital, and it is this autonomy that grants it a particular power, relative to those private capitals. Keynesianism - the idea that states can intervene to smooth out the cycle of boom and bust - is a dramatic assertion of this autonomy, requiring a state to boost spending when all other capitalists are cutting theirs, and vice versa.

The relationship between the state and private capitals tends to set the terrain for the key debates within capitalist society about how the economy should function. Since the crisis of the 1970s, a particular form of that debate (and its associated ideology) has come to dominate. This is neoliberalism, which, at the level of ideology, has stressed the independence of private capital from the state. In reality, this has involved a subordination of the state to private capital, clamping down on the autonomy present under Keynesianism, and (most dramatically) the emphasis on the financial system as the leading element of capitalism.

Finance grew under capitalism in a similar manner to the state, acting as a means, initially, to try and provide some order and planning to the system. By taking value from many different sources, the financial system as a whole can attempt to provide more effective investments for capitalists, particularly as the system expands beyond the point at which individual capitalists or even firms can reasonably know how and where to invest. Like the state, it can enjoy a degree of autonomy from capitalist accumulation; like the state, as capital becomes more 'concentrated' (grows bigger), its role becomes more important.

The financial system has been transformed in the last thirty years. The ending of deliberate state controls on finance (and international flows of finance in particular), combined with a loosening of regulations on state controls of money, have allowed the financial system to expand enormously relative to the wider economy. Flows of international finance have (at least until 2008) far outweighed the growth of international trade, which was, itself, prodigious over this period as Western capital expanded into areas previously excluded from its orbit, and parts of the older 'Third World', notably in East Asia, rapidly industrialised.

The logic of finance is close to a 'pure' logic of capitalism, stripped of the nuisance of production. It is simply:

$$M-M'$$

In other words, money producing more money. Of course, at some point, the expansion of value that this growth in money represents has to be actualised: new value must be produced, finance cannot literally produce value out of nowhere. Exploitation still grounds the system. For a while, aided by state management of the interest rate and other controls on financial activity, the expansion of finance can seemingly continue without reference to the real economy. The boom of the 2000s had this character, particularly in the UK, with the growth of financial liabilities (debts) far outstripping the growth of the wider economy, measured in terms of income growth. Of course this set up was not sustainable, however clever the financiers thought they were being, and it was the state that stepped in very directly - through the notorious bailouts - when the debacle erupted in 2008. Finance can appear autonomous, just like the state, but is always forced by the logic of capitalism back into line with the rest of the economy. The state and finance between them have tied themselves together in increasingly complex fashion, particularly as the opportunities for exploitation and the production of surplus value (at least in the West) seem harder to come by.

Capitalism is, in Marx's description, a competitive and exploitative system that has little to do with meeting genuine human needs. It lurches unthinkingly into crises and, as it expands, it becomes more, not less, erratic and irrational. There is no solution to this irrationality, in the end, without ending capitalism itself.

4. Marx and Revolution

Katherine Connelly

'There is no alternative' is the mantra of neoliberal capitalism. For decades we have been told that the answer to the problems of capitalism was more capitalism. Everything imaginable could and should be privatised, from railways, water, electricity - even directory enquiries did not escape. The capitalists themselves knew what was best for capitalism so they ought to be freed from the 'interference' of democracy; Gordon Brown, who championed further deregulation of the banks, declared the end of boom and bust. Then, in 2008, the boom burst - and in the most deregulated centres of capitalism - starting in the most capitalist of nations, the United States.

The ruling ideas of our ruling class were exposed as wholly unable to explain the crisis of its own system. In the decades of smug neoliberal certainties, the ideas of Karl Marx had been derided as irrelevant and discredited. However, after the financial crash of 2008 Marx's ideas on economics were to some extent rehabilitated; his writings on capitalism were discussed in the most surprising of places - in BBC documentaries and the columns of the *Financial Times* - and Marx's bearded face began to make an appearance on book covers in bestseller displays in bookshops.

The rehabilitation was, however, strictly partial. Karl Marx, it was conceded, might have had some useful things to say about economics, and thus his works were desperately consulted for an explanation of the crisis, but there was no concession given to Marx's solution. Those rehabilitating Marx continued to regard his ideas about revolution as utopian, unrealistic and dangerous. They continued to promote the idea that ordinary people do not have the capacity to organise society any better; indeed we are constantly told that should we dare to attempt to do so we would only make it worse for ourselves.

The argument is so familiar we can all recite it unprompted: ordinary people might participate in a revolution with the best of intentions but they would end up creating a system in which a small elite would rule at the expense of the many. (How telling that the nightmare future we are warned to avoid at all costs appears so achingly contemporary and familiar!) Trite comments are mobilised in support of this argument purporting to summarise universal human behaviour: human beings are too selfish. The evidence, we are told, is all around us: capitalism is a system that reflects our essential greedy selfishness; we are so implicated in our own suffering that we cannot be capable of rejecting it.

This attempt to present capitalism as an eternal and natural system was as recognisable to Marx as it is to us. In one of his most famous and polemical works, *The Communist Manifesto*, Marx confronted this argument, addressing the dominant capitalist class directly:

> *The selfish misconception that induces you to transform into eternal laws of nature and reason, the social forms springing from your present mode of production and form of property – historical relations that rise and disappear in the progress of production – this misconception you share with every ruling class that has preceded you.*[1]

The sting – for the capitalists – is in the tail; as Marx recalled, that there have been other systems, with different modes of production and forms of property, that also thought themselves eternal before they themselves were usurped by capitalism. Capitalism is not, then, eternal; it is not the inevitable result of 'human nature'. It has a history; it was born, and what can be born can also die. Moreover, it was the bourgeois revolutions, from the English Revolution of the 1640s, the American War of Independence from the 1770s to the 1780s, and most decisively the French Revolution of 1789, which overwhelmed the power of the feudal elites, enabling capitalism's own rise to dominance.

Revolution is far from a historical aberration; it is capitalism's guilty secret. In the same way, revolution was not an afterthought, nor a glib solution that Marx artificially imposed after he had done his sophisticated thinking on economics. Revolution was central to Marx's whole life.

The Communist Manifesto, written in 1848 when Marx was thirty years old, concludes that human emancipation can only be achieved by a revolutionary overthrow of capitalism, and therefore revolution must be the goal of the activists he was writing for:

> *Communists distain to conceal their views and aims. They openly declare that their ends can be attained only by the forcible overthrow of all existing social conditions. Let the ruling classes tremble at a Communistic revolution.*[2]

At Marx's funeral in 1883 Friedrich Engels, his lifelong friend, collaborator and co-author of the *Manifesto*, delivered the oration at the graveside in Highgate Cemetery in which he emphasised how fundamental revolution was to Marx's life's work:

> *For Marx was before all else a revolutionist. His real mission in life was to contribute, in one way or another, to the overthrow of capitalist society and of the state institutions which it had brought into being, to contribute to the liberation of the modern proletariat, which he was the first to make conscious of its own position and its needs, conscious of the conditions of its emancipation. Fighting was his element. And he fought with a passion, a tenacity and a success such as few could rival.*

Karl Marx without revolution is nothing but wishful thinking on the part of today's capitalists scrabbling around for a capitalist solution to a capitalist crisis. Revolution was integral to and inseparable from Marx's understanding of history, economics and politics.

The limits of bourgeois revolution

Marx did not subscribe to a theory of history as unfolding according to a divine plan, or through the actions of a few great individuals (as it is still often taught today). Marx understood great historical changes as driven by the class struggles between the people with power and the people without: the outcomes of struggles between slaves against slave-owners, serfs against lords, capitalists against feudal society, shaped human history. Most of the time those with power remained victorious, but at times the class struggle intensified into revolutionary struggles against the old order, in which all the previously established norms of society were challenged.

This had happened in what Marx termed the bourgeois revolutions in which the capitalist class (or bourgeoisie) revolted against the old feudal structures which were stifling the expansionist and innovative economic activity that capitalism depended upon to survive. However, the bourgeoisie were not numerically large enough to overthrow the old regimes on their own, and relied upon an alliance with other sections of society far lower down the social and economic scale, who had reasons enough of their own to want to see the end of the feudal order.

This temporary alliance led to tensions within the revolutions, between those who sought to appoint themselves the new ruling class, and those who had made the revolution because they wanted to see far-reaching social changes. In the English Revolution radical groups such as the Levellers and whole sections of the rank and file of the army that fought against the King struggled for greater democratic changes than the new elite in Parliament and the top of the army led by Oliver Cromwell were prepared to concede. In the French Revolution, the *sans culottes*, those who had stormed the Bastille and made the revolution, soon found themselves in conflict with the middle-class politicians who dominated the National Assembly. Writing in the 1840s, Marx predicted that in the next bourgeois revolution, which he believed would break out in Germany, the contradictions between the bourgeois minority and the mass of revolutionary participants would become uncontainable and would thus swiftly lead to a second revolution led by the working-class (or proletariat).

In 1848 revolutions broke out across Europe as people in France, Belgium, the German states, the Italian states, and the Austro-Hungarian Empire rose up against their rulers. Marx and Engels, who had been living abroad, hastened back to their native Germany to participate. The tensions between the bourgeois leaders of the revolution and the aspirations of the revolutionary workers did indeed result in conflict between these groups, but it was in Paris, rather than in Germany, that this conflict first broke out. The result would seal the fate of the revolutions across the continent.

In Paris, revolutionary workers demanded that the new government enable the urban poor to share in the gains of the revolution by establishing national workshops to provide paid work for the unemployed. The majority in the government were deeply uncomfortable with this radical social experiment and in June 1848 they announced the closure of the national workshops. The working-class quarters of Paris rose in insurrection and the barricades were rebuilt. Now a journalist writing for the German revolutionaries, Marx championed the 'June Days' uprising as the dawn of the proletarian revolution. However, the fate of the June insurrection would in fact demonstrate for all to see that the bourgeoisie would sooner turn to counter-revolution. They would prefer to destroy the gains even of their own revolution rather than allow a successful workers' revolution.

The response of the bourgeois French government was uncompromisingly brutal, drowning the workers' insurrection in its own blood. They sent troops into the working-class districts, where over three days they bombarded barricades and homes alike. Thousands were slaughtered on the streets of Paris and thousands more were deported to Algeria in the aftermath. In the months that followed, important and powerful sections of the bourgeoisie, from politicians to newspaper editors, turned to Louis Napoleon Bonaparte, nephew of Napoleon I, to save the revolution from itself. Louis Napoleon, whose dictatorial ambitions were well-known, was elected President at the end of 1848 and seized dictatorial power in a coup d'état three years later, abolishing all the democratic gains of the revolution.

Louis Napoleon's pompously proclaimed 'Second Empire' was characterised by rampant capitalist development. He brought in Baron Haussmann who created a new imperial capital, workers' houses were demolished and their inhabitants driven to the outskirts of the city, and the old narrow streets so well-suited to barricade-building were demolished to make way for the wide boulevards. Paris became the home of fashion and huge department stores, and the railway network was rapidly expanded, with railway stations built as monuments to national glory. Paris, in the words of the critic Walter Benjamin, became 'the capital of the nineteenth century'.

The course of the 1848 revolution in France had shown that when faced with the prospect of a workers' revolution, the bourgeoisie prioritised saving capitalism above saving democracy. In *The Eighteenth Brumaire of Louis Bonaparte*, written in the immediate aftermath of Louis Napoleon's seizure of power, Marx evocatively characterised this as history repeating itself first as tragedy, the second time as farce. Marx deployed this metaphor throughout the book to expose the rhetoric of contemporary bourgeois revolutions: they were claiming to stand in the heroic revolutionary tradition of 1789 but, whereas the former bourgeois revolution had played a progressive role in history, the revolution of 1848 was hindering, even physically crushing, historical progress. Thus its claims to heroism were nothing but a lifeless, embarrassing parody of what had gone before. The biggest joke of all was that 1848 even had its own mediocre Napoleon in place of the formidable Napoleon of the past.

The bourgeoisie was no longer the insurgent class as in 1789, but a ruling class desperately clinging on to its power, and therefore it could no longer play a progressive revolutionary role. After 1848, Marx concluded, the working class could only hope to achieve its emancipation if it consciously articulated its own independent revolutionary demands that openly challenged the power of the bourgeoisie.

Revolutionary gravediggers

Crucially, however, the working class was not reliant upon bourgeois action to inspire hostility and resistance to capitalism. Marx insisted that the very structure of capitalism itself produced this. In *The Communist Manifesto*, Marx described the tendency of capitalism to divide society increasingly into two camps: the property owners, who owned the means of production (the bourgeoisie) and those without property, who sold their labour to the bourgeoisie and produced everything (the proletariat or working class). Although working-class labour was the source of all the unprecedented wealth under capitalism, most of the wealth was taken as profit by the bourgeois company owner before it ever got near the worker's pay packet. The precious little that was left was soon taken afterwards by other capitalists, the landlords who charged rent and the businessmen who sold commodities to workers at a price that ensured a handsome profit for themselves.

This system of exploitation led to workers demanding a share in the wealth that they created, and these demands were only strengthened as developing industry gathered increasingly large numbers of workers into huge factories. These changes were initially most evident in Britain, the most industrialised country in Europe and home of the 'dark, satanic mills' that haunted the poet William Blake. Workers, who were organised to work collectively to produce goods, began to self-organise collectively, forming trade unions, to press for changes to their conditions of work. This did far more than anger individual employers; the response of the state to the birth of trade unionism demonstrated the extent to which this was seen as a potential threat to the entire social order. The Combination Acts, passed at the turn of the nineteenth century, made trade unionism illegal and though they were finally repealed in 1824, a new Act of Parliament was passed a year later severely restricting trade union activities. In 1834, six agricultural workers in the rural village of Tolpuddle were sentenced to transportation to Australia for daring to form a trade union.

These experiences forced many trade unionists to conclude that the implications of their struggle went far beyond confronting individual employers and fighting for changes in individual workplaces; the entire political system had to be changed so that working people could have a say in the way society was organised. Arriving in Manchester, the heart of the Industrial Revolution, in 1842 Friedrich Engels observed the way in which collective resistance to working conditions fed into political and social struggles against a deeply unequal society. Engels quickly made contact with the Chartist movement, a mass working-class movement demanding sweeping political reform, which had, in the year of his arrival, organised a general strike that had threatened to turn into a full-blown insurrection.

Capitalism, Marx argued, had in fact produced its own gravediggers. Workers had no stake in the existing system, since they did not have property. They had no great reserves of wealth and nor were they in any position to accumulate any, and, unlike the emerging capitalist class under feudal society, their existence was not based upon the exploitation of any other group of people in society. The rallying cry at the end of the *Manifesto* alludes precisely to this: 'The proletarians have nothing to lose but their chains'.[4] Working-class revolution, then, would not be a revolution conducted in the narrow interest of a particular group against the interests of others, in fact it was precisely the conditions that capitalism had imposed upon its workers that would make a workers' revolution fundamentally different from all the previous revolutions:

> *All previous historical movements were movements of minorities, or in the interests of minorities. The proletarian movement is the self-conscious, independent movement of the immense majority, in the interest of the immense majority. The proletariat, the lowest stratum of our present society, cannot stir, cannot raise itself up, without the whole superincumbent strata of official society being sprung into the air.*[5]

Therefore, the emancipation of the working class would be the emancipation of more than itself alone. It was for this reason that Marx described it as 'the class that holds the future in its hands'. Moreover, the emancipation of the working class could only be achieved through a revolution which smashed the existing state and created society anew. Workers would be unable to achieve their emancipation while the existing system was intact because that very system was wholly dependent upon the exploitation of the working class.

This was the important precedent that Marx saw in the establishment of a workers' government in Paris in 1871. The fall of Napoleon III's empire in the Franco-Prussian War of 1870 saw the declaration of a republican government in France, which then sparked a working-class uprising in Paris when that new government attempted to disarm the workers who had been defending the city from the Prussian army. The republican government fled the capital and the revolutionary workers declared a Paris Commune.

The Paris Commune would exist only for 72 days before it was mercilessly crushed by the republican government it had humiliated, but in its short-lived existence it constructed a state on radically new principles which placed democratic power in the hands of the people. Marx assessed that the achievement of the Commune had been to demonstrate that 'the working class cannot simply lay hold of the ready-made State machinery, and wield it for its own purposes'.[6] Representatives in the Commune were not only elected by the people, the people also had the right to recall them if they felt they were not effectively representing their interests, this principle applied not only to members of the revolutionary government, but also to the judiciary. The standing army was abolished and replaced by a National Guard and the police were made accountable to the Commune. Huge social changes, that would take bourgeois governments decades if not centuries to achieve (if at all), were effected in these few short weeks. Amongst the many measures passed was the separation of Church and state, public servants to be paid workers' wages, the abolition of the death penalty, the introduction of free, and compulsory education for girls as well as boys, with equal pay for male and female teachers.

Ideas to change the world

Marx developed his ideas about revolution in response to the real events, dilemmas and debates that took place in his own time. Famously he wanted not only to interpret the world but to change it. He placed such a central importance on drawing the correct conclusions from events because he understood that although capitalism inevitably produced its own antithesis, in the form of the working class, capitalist society expended great ideological effort to prevent workers from appreciating their own power and from identifying their enemy. Therefore, while capitalism puts workers in the workplace together, it also seeks to drive them apart, to dispel any sense of unity, by pitting workers against each other in the labour market. Some workers are kept unemployed, they are paid at different rates and are forced to compete for jobs. On top of this, we are bombarded with the language of division by employers, politicians, and the media who constantly tell us that our enemy is not the boss but other workers, immigrants, women, gay people, the disabled, travellers, asylum seekers, people on benefits… the list seems endless.

Marx understood the devastating power of ruling class ideas and did not believe they could be effectively challenged on an individual basis. Throughout his life he was a member of revolutionary organisations: when he wrote *The Communist Manifesto* he was a member of the Communist League, and in the 1860s he was a founding member of the International Workingmen's Association. Marx and Engels were in constant contact with other radicals and revolutionaries, discussing and arguing with them about ideas and strategies. They understood that the ideas held by the revolutionary actors would be a decisive factor in the fate of that action. More ardent than Marx's desire to see a revolution, was his desire to see a successful revolution; he had seen the terrible price of failed, incomplete and defeated revolutions time and again. Unlike so many intellectuals, Marx did not separate his ideas from practice; he wrote to assist revolutionaries. Today, Marx's writings do far more than help explain the world as it is, they help us understand that we can and must change it.

Notes

1. Marx and Engels (2002) *The Communist Manifesto*, London: Penguin Books, p.239.
2. Ibid, p.258.
3. https://www.marxists.org/archive/marx/works/1883/death/burial.htm
4. Marx and Engels (2002) *The Communist Manifesto*, London: Penguin Books, p.258.
5. Ibid, p.232.
6. Marx and Engels (1986) *Collected Works*, Volume 22, London: Lawrence and Wishart, p.238.

Further reading

Karl Marx
The Communist Manifesto
The German Ideology
Wage Labour and Capital
Value, Price and Profit

Terry Eagleton
Why Marx Was Right

Ben Fine and Alfredo Saad Filho
Marx's Capital

Franz Jakubowski
Ideology and Superstructure

Lindsey German, 'Reflections on the Communist Manifesto', https://www.marxists.org/history/etol/writers/german/1998/xx/manifesto.htm

John Rees, 'The Socialist Revolution and the Democratic Revolution', https://www.marxists.org/history/etol/writers/rees-j/1999/xx/revolution.htm

About the authors

Lindsey German

As national convenor of the Stop the War Coalition, Lindsey German was a key organiser of the largest demonstration, and one of the largest mass movements, in British history. Her books include *Material Girls: Women, Men and Work*; *Sex, Class and Socialism*; *A People's History of London* (with John Rees); and *How a Century of War Changed the Lives of Women*.

Chris Nineham

Chris Nineham is a founder member of the Stop the War Coalition and Counterfire, speaking regularly around the country on behalf of both. He is author of *The People V. Tony Blair* and *Capitalism and Class Consciousness: The Ideas of Georg Lukacs*.

James Meadway

Senior economist at the New Economics Foundation, James Meadway has been an important critic of austerity-economics and is at the forefront of efforts to promulgate an alternative. He is co-author of *Crisis in the Eurozone* and the *How to Run the Country Manual*.

Katherine Connelly

Katherine Connelly is a writer and historian. She led school student strikes in the British anti-war movement in 2003, co-ordinated the Emily Wilding Davison Memorial Campaign in 2013 and is a leading member of Counterfire. She is the author of *Sylvia Pankhurst: Suffragette, Socialist and Scourge of Empire*.

COUNTERFIRE

Counterfire is a socialist organisation dedicated to building the movements against war, austerity, racism, Islamophobia, and climate change. We believe that fundamental change can only come from below, but that it requires socialist organisation.

We want to see a left that can make a real difference to the world. There are Counterfire groups around the country that are central to the People's Assemblies Against Austerity, to the anti-war movement and many other campaigns.

Help remake socialist politics for the 21st century. Join us, we are stronger together: www.counterfire.org/join